WORLD RELIGIONS

Hinduism

Katherine Prior

W
FRANKLIN WATTS
LONDON•SYDNEY

First published in 1999 by Franklin Watts
96 Leonard Street, London EC2A 4XD

Franklin Watts Australia
14 Mars Road, Lane Cove
NSW 2066

© Franklin Watts 1999

Editor: Sarah Snashall
Art director: Robert Walster
Designer: Simon Borrough
Picture research: Sue Mennell

Religious consultants:
Mr Krishan Bhatia, journalist and
President of Shree Vishwa Hindu
Mandir, Southall
Angela Wood, teacher, broadcaster and
curriculum adviser in religious education
Lesley Prior, advisory teacher and
lecturer in religious education

A CIP catalogue record for this book is
available from the British Library.

ISBN 0 7496 3376 X

Dewey classification 294.5

Printed in Hong Kong/China

Picture credits:

Cover: Format (Raissa Page); James Davis Travel
Photography (inset).

AKG/Jean-Louis Nou p. 9b;
Axiom/Jim Holmes p.28;
Christine Oxborne Pictures pp. 5b, 19t, 26, 27t,
e. t. archive/Victoria and Albert Museum pp. 10,
11l, 13b, 31;
Eye Ubiquitous pp. 12t (Pam Smith),
14t (David Peez), 15 (David Cohen),
16 (Adina Tovy Amsel), 21b (Bennett Dean),
22 (David Cumming), 23b (Bennett Dean),
23t (David Cumming), 27b (Patrick Bouineau),
29 (Jason Burke);
Format pp. 5t (Raissa Page), 14b (Judy Harrison);
Images of India Picture Agency pp. 13t
(S. D. Manchekar/DPA),
24t (Jagdish Agrawal/DPA), 25 (MMN/DPA);
Impact pp. 4 (Mike McQueen), 9t (Mark Henley),
19b (Francesco Rizzoli), 21t (Alain Evrard);
James Davis Travel Photography p.7t
Panos Pictures pp. 7b (Börje Tobiasson),
20 (DAS), 24b (Ron Giling),
28t (Alison Wright);
Ann and Bury Peerless pp. 8, 11r;
Steve Shott pp. 6, 12b, 17 (both), 18.

CONTENTS

THE SUPREME BEING   4

LIFE AND DEATH   6

SACRED WRITINGS   8

LORD VISHNU AND HIS AVATARS   10

LORD SHIVA AND PARVATI   12

BHAKTI: LOVE OF THE LORD   14

HINDU TEMPLES   16

PUJA   18

HOLY DAYS AND FESTIVALS   20

PILGRIMAGE   22

VARNAS   24

DHARMA: AN IDEAL LIFE   26

CEREMONIES FOR LIFE   28

IMPORTANT DATES   30

GLOSSARY   31

INDEX   32

THE SUPREME BEING

HINDUS BELIEVE IN THE ONE SUPREME BEING who created everything. The Supreme Being contains every characteristic of the universe and it is both male and female, beautiful and ugly, creative and destructive, all and nothing.

Hindus believe it is impossible for humans to grasp fully the Supreme Being, and they have created thousands of gods and goddesses to express the Supreme Being's characteristics. Many Hindus worship a local god who has special powers in their area, as well as a major god who is worshipped by Hindus throughout the world.

In a temple in south India images of the main Hindu gods and goddesses stand around a sacred fire.

The Triad

There are three great gods in Hinduism: Brahma, Vishnu and Shiva. Together these gods represent the powers of creation, preservation and destruction which maintain the universe.

There are thousands of other gods and goddesses including the popular gods Krishna and Rama.

A Hindu girl and her friends in Britain join in the festival which celebrates the story of the god Rama.

A Hindu priest lights a ghee lamp before an image of Vishnu.

Varnas

Most Hindus are born into a Hindu family. They are born into one of four main groups called *varnas*. These groups are the Brahmins, the Kshatriyas, the Vaishyas and the Sudras. Below the four *varnas* are the Untouchables.

Today, some Hindus do not accept the system of *varnas*.

The Hindu priesthood

Hinduism has no central authority which appoints priests. Most priests are Brahmin men but there are many different types, such as temple priests, funeral priests and pilgrimage priests. Each new priest is the son or nephew of an existing priest. He is taught the necessary sacred texts and rituals by his older male relations and when they die he inherits their priesthood.

Hinduism around the world

Hinduism is the main religion of India. It began in India at least years 3,500 years ago and is one of the oldest religions in the world, much older than Buddhism, Christianity or Islam.

Hindus have taken their religion with them when they have emigrated from India. Today there are large Hindu communities in Singapore, Mauritius, the Caribbean, East and South Africa, Canada, the USA, Britain and Australia.

5

LIFE AND DEATH

IN HINDUISM, time does not run in a straight line, but in cycles. Over millions of years the universe is created, exists and is then destroyed, before being created all over again. For all living things, life follows the same cycle of birth, death and rebirth. Being born again and again on earth is called reincarnation. The physical body is destroyed at death, but the soul returns to earth in a new body.

This woman improves her *karma* for the next life by praying. Prayer is a form of *puja*.

Karma: inheritance from past lives

Hindus do not know who they were in a previous life, but they believe that their actions in a previous life affect their current life. This is called *karma*. It loosely means fate. A poor man may say that it is his *karma* which keeps him poor; he may believe he is being punished in his current life for irreligious behaviour in a previous life.

Certain is death for all those born and certain is birth for all those dead; Therefore over the inevitable you should not grieve.

Bhagavad Gita, II, 27.

Moksha: liberation from the cycle of rebirths

Every Hindu aims to break the cycle of rebirths and achieve *moksha* – freedom from the sufferings and desires of life. *Moksha* is a state of nothingness, where a person no longer feels pain, joy or sadness. After death they are not reborn again because their soul has been absorbed by the Supreme Being.

Hindus try to achieve *moksha* by living a holy life. If they do not achieve *moksha* in this life, they know that by their good actions they have improved their *karma* for the next life.

This Hindu holy man, or *sadhu*, devotes himself to prayer to achieve *moksha*.

These women are walking hundreds of miles to visit a holy site. Going on a pilgrimage is a form of *puja*.

Puja: worship

Hindus express their devotion to a god or goddesss through worship. The basic act of worship in Hinduism is called *puja*.

Hindus also believe that performing *puja* earns them religious merit with their god. It is like a blessing from the god for their holy behaviour. They can use this religious merit for help in their current lives, such as the cure of an illness, or they can save it for when they die in the hope of achieving *moksha*.

7

SACRED WRITINGS

THE EARLIEST KNOWN WRITINGS OF HINDUISM are a collection of hymns and prayers, called the Vedas. Veda is a Sanskrit word meaning 'knowledge'. The first of the Vedas is the *Rig Veda*. It probably began to be written down in about 1300BCE, but it existed in people's memories before that.

Krishna appears as a chariot-driver, before Arjuna.

The *Mahabharata*

Many other sacred texts were created after the Vedas, including the two epics of the *Mahabharata* and the *Ramayana*.

The *Mahabharata* tells of the long struggle by the Pandavas, five princely brothers, to regain their kingdom from the Kauravas, their evil cousins. There are many exciting battles in the *Mahabharata*, but its most famous part is a chapter called the *Bhagavad Gita,* or Song of the Lord – in which the god Krishna advises Arjuna, the chief Pandava, on good and evil and the right way to behave in life. Many Hindus today use the *Bhagavad Gita* as their guide to daily behaviour.

Fix thy mind on Me; be devoted to Me; sacrifice unto Me; bow down to Me; Having thus united thy whole self with Me, taking me as the Supreme Goal, thou shalt come unto Me.

Bhagavad Gita, IX, 34.

The *Ramayana*

Hinduism's other major epic, the *Ramayana*, tells the story of the god Rama. Rama is king of Ayodhya, but he gives up his kingdom following the wishes of his father. He wanders around India with his wife Sita and his brother Lakshman, but Sita is kidnapped by Ravana, the ten-headed demon-king of Lanka. Rama and Lakshman call on the help of Hanuman, a god in the form of a monkey, to kill Ravana and win Sita back.

Like the *Mahabharata*, the *Ramayana* is an exciting story, but it contains serious lessons about duty, honour and correct behaviour.

A man reads a sacred book at dawn by the River Ganges as part of his daily worship.

In the *Ramayana*, Hanuman helps Rama win back Sita.

The language of Sanskrit

The Vedas and the *Mahabharata* and *Ramayana* were first written in Sanskrit, an ancient language which was once widely known throughout India. Today most Hindus read the holy books in translation.

Lord Vishnu and his Avatars

Hindus think of all the gods in Hinduism as different expressions of the Supreme Being, but they usually worship one main god. Vishnu is one of the most popular. He is the creator and preserver of the universe and is merciful to humans. Vishnu's wife is Lakshmi, the goddess of wealth and good luck.

Here, Vishnu is shown as the whole world. He carries a white conch shell, a lotus flower, and two weapons.

For the protection of the good, for the destruction of the wicked and for the establishment of righteousness, I come into being in every age.

Bhagavad Gita, IV, 8.

Vishnu comes to earth

Vishnu has visited earth nine times to crush evil and to restore divine order. Each time he has come as a different being, called an avatar. Vaishnavites (Vishnu worshippers) believe that Vishnu will make a tenth and final visit to earth at the ending of this world.

Two of Vishnu's avatars are very important: the seventh one, Rama, and the eighth one, Krishna. There are thousands of temples dedicated to Rama and Krishna.

Lord Rama

Rama is the hero of the *Ramayana*. Vishnu came to earth in the form of Rama to defeat Ravana, the demon-king of Lanka, who was threatening to destroy the world. Every year in the Hindu month of Ashvin (September-October) Hindus observe the festival of Dussehra which celebrates the triumph of good over evil. During Dussehra worshippers of Rama recite the *Ramayana* and act out its story.

Using the magic snake, Shesha, Vishnu orders demons and gods to stir the ocean to keep the world in harmony.

In plays of the *Ramayana*, huge models of Ravana are exploded with fireworks.

Lord Krishna

After his appearance as Rama, Vishnu next came to earth as Krishna to defeat the demon Kansa. Krishna-worshippers love the stories of his childhood which tell of a mischievous, fun-loving god. In pictures he is shown as a chubby baby stealing butter, or as a handsome young cowherd with a flute, playing with the *gopis* – the milkmaids who fell in love with him. Krishna in this form, as well as the wise god of the *Bhagavad Gita*, is popular among Vaishnavites.

LORD SHIVA AND PARVATI

SHIVA IS THE GOD WHO OCCASIONALLY destroys the universe in order for it to be born again. Shiva can be a frightening god, who may unleash his immense power at any time.

A Shaivite monk, who worships Shiva and his family, is known by Shiva's symbols: a trident and unkempt hair.

Protector and destroyer

Shiva can use his power to preserve as well as to destroy. When the gods dropped the sacred River Ganges from the heavens, Shiva caught the mighty waters in his hair to slow them down and prevent them from washing away the earth.

A *murti* of Lord Shiva in a temple.

The perfect monk

Shiva's tangled hair is the symbol of a *yogi*, a Hindu monk, and he is often pictured as the perfect monk. As a god of opposites, however, Shiva is not only a monk. He has a beautiful wife, Parvati, and two sons, one of whom is Ganesha.

Ganesha

Ganesha has an elephant's head. When he was a young man, his father, Shiva, mistook him for a stranger entering his house and chopped off his head in a rage. Horrified to learn that he had killed his own son, Shiva used the head of the nearest animal – an elephant – to bring him back to life.

Ganesha is the remover of obstacles, he can make things go smoothly, or – if he is ignored – badly. He is associated with beginnings. He guards entrances and his image is to be found by the door of Hindu homes and temples.

At a festival in Bombay in western India, an image of Ganesha is taken to the ocean to be bathed.

The Great Goddess

There are many goddesses in Hinduism. All are different versions of the one Great Goddess, called Mahadevi or Shakti. Shakti means power.

One of the most powerful goddesses is Kali. Like Shiva, Kali is a goddess of destruction and death. However, Kali's worshippers also see her as a figure of life. For Hindus, just as death must follow life, so life must follow death.

A painting of Kali from the Kalighat Temple, Calcutta, shows her with a necklace of severed heads dripping blood.

13

BHAKTI: LOVE OF THE LORD

IN THE EARLY CENTURIES of Hinduism, religious knowledge was strictly controlled by the priests. There were many sacrifices which were expensive to perform and were restricted to men of the top three castes or *varnas*. Women and poor or low-caste men were shut out from the religious ceremonies.

Hindu gods can be worshipped with simple offerings of garlands of flowers.

These women are singing hymns of love and devotion to their god.

The beginnings of devotional worship

In about the 6th century CE, there was a reaction against this form of Hinduism. Beginning in south India, religious teachers began to say that all Hindus could approach their god directly with prayers, hymns and simple, inexpensive offerings, such as flowers. The important thing was that the worshippers, no matter how humble and poor, should love their god with absolute devotion.

This powerful movement was called *bhakti* and it spread all over India, especially among Hindus who worshipped Rama and Krishna. As many Hindus rejected the right of the Brahmin priests to tell them how to worship, they demanded holy books in their own languages rather than just the priestly language of Sanskrit.

Kabir: a poet saint

Many new hymns and prayers were written by people from *varnas* which were considered low at that time. One such poet was Kabir (1440–1518CE), a weaver from the city of Varanasi. He wrote poems in simple language which urged Hindus to be pure, humble and loving. He attacked the rules about *varna* and the power of the priests.

Bhakti-marga: the Way of Devotion

Even though it began so long ago, this form of worship is still practised by millions of Hindus. It is called *bhakti-marga*, the Way of Devotion. Hymn-singing, prayers, making offerings and gazing on the image of a god are all parts of *bhakti-marga*. *Bhakti-marga* stresses the love of all living things and its followers are often vegetarians who are against killing animals.

A man takes time out of his working day to pray in the sacred River Ganges.

HINDU TEMPLES

HINDUS MAKE MANY IMAGES of the gods they worship. These images, called *murtis*, can be any size. When the image of a god is finished, a priest holds a ceremony to ask the god to enter it. Until this ceremony has been performed, the image is simply a sculpture with no religious meaning.

The god at the centre of the universe

A god's image should have a proper house. This may be a grand temple or a tiny shrine in a family's home. Temples, also called *mandirs*, are square or rectangular in shape, often surrounded by a strong outer wall. Inside there are halls built one inside the other. The outside rooms are beautifully decorated, but at the very centre of the temple is a small, plain room, lit only by flickering oil lamps. This is where the main god sits.

The temple represents the universe. The god's position in the dark central chamber shows the god to be at the centre of creation, with the world spreading out from him or her.

Most Hindu temples, like this one in England, have a tall tower under which the main god sits.

Other gods

Other gods are arranged in the rooms coming off from the central chamber. The outer rooms in the temple are used by the temple's priests, servants and musicians, and sometimes by pilgrims and monks.

A worshipper rings a temple bell to tell the god that he is approaching.

Children pray in a temple.

Visiting the temple

Visitors to a temple enter through the main gateway and then walk through all the rooms in a clockwise direction, passing all of the lesser gods before they reach the central room where the main god sits. It is disrespectful to approach the god in an anticlockwise direction. Near the central room there is a bell for them to strike to tell the god of their approach. The worshippers enter the central room and stand before the god.

ॐ PUJA

Puja, or worship, can be performed in a temple or at a shrine at home. In *puja* at a temple, worshippers give their offerings to the priest who offers them to the god. The offerings may be flowers, fruits, milk, sweets, incense or money.

Prasad: holy gifts from the god

A priest pours holy liquid, *prasad*, into the hands of a girl.

Any liquid offerings are poured over the image of the god. The liquid runs off the image and is collected in sacred pots. The priest pours the holy liquid into the worshippers' cupped hands. They drink it and sprinkle their hair with any drops that remain. Any offerings of flowers and sweets are returned to the worshippers.

All the returned offerings are called *prasad*. Hindus believe that the god has consumed their offerings and is now returning them filled with religious power and grace.

Darshan: seeing the god

As well as *prasad*, during *puja* a worshipper should receive *darshan*. *Darshan* is the experience of making eye contact with the god's image. Worshippers press their hands together beneath their chin. Then looking eye to eye with the god they make their prayers and requests. *Darshan* is the time of most private contact between Hindus and their god.

After *puja*, Hindus often use ash or powder to mark their foreheads with the sign of their god.

During *puja* a woman prays and makes eye contact with the image of her god.

Mother cow

Temple priests perform a series of *pujas* before the god's image every day. Some of these use the five sacred products of the cow: milk, curds, ghee (purified butter), dung and urine. The cow's products are sacred because she is worshipped by Hindus as the source of nourishment and the symbol of life. It is wrong to harm or kill a cow, and devout Hindus will never eat beef.

Cows are decorated for a festival which offers thanks for the food and labour they give to people.

Holy days and festivals

Hinduism has hundreds of holy days and religious celebrations. Two of the most popular are Diwali and Holi.

A schoolgirl paints a Diwali lamp on the window of her classroom.

A girl paints a pattern on a friend's hand during Diwali.

Diwali

Diwali falls in the Hindu month of Kartik (October-November) when new winter crops are about to be sown in India. On the evening of Diwali, Hindus worship Lakshmi, the goddess of wealth, beauty and good luck. They leave out a lamp full of ghee to welcome her into their lives for the coming year. Hindus set off fireworks to frighten away evil spirits and light up their houses and shops with thousands of tiny oil lamps, candles or electric bulbs.

Wearing their new clothes, families set out to exchange sweets with their friends and neighbours and wish them good luck for the coming year.

Holi

Holi is one of the most colourful festivals in Hinduism. It falls in the month of Phalgun (February-March), when it is spring in India. It celebrates energy, vitality and youthful mischief.

Bright flags and saris decorate a fishing boat in Bombay during the Holi festival.

Holi occurs over two days. On the evening of the first day, a bamboo and straw statue of Holika, a child-eating witch, is placed in the centre of a bonfire and burnt to the ground. Early next morning, people flock into the streets and spray coloured powders and inks over each other. Until noon, all the normal rules are broken: children can squirt their parents with paint; workers can insult their bosses. In the evening, people exchange sweets and friends embrace each other three times and wish each other good luck. Children touch the feet of their parents and grandparents to show their respect and to prove that things are now back to normal.

These men have been happily spraying each other with paint and coloured powders during Holi.

PILGRIMAGE

HINDUS BELIEVE that the Supreme Being is present all around them, but they recognize some places as being especially sacred because a god is directly connected with them.

A crossing place

These sacred places are called *tirthas*. At a *tirtha* the religious power is so strong that one can cross over from the ordinary world to the home of the gods.

All *tirthas* have water nearby, either a river or a large pool. Water is a sacred substance in Hinduism because it can flow between the earth and the home of the gods.

Thousands of Hindus bathe at the sacred city of Varanasi (Kashi) every morning.

Famous pilgrimage sites

Three of Hinduism's most famous pilgrimage sites are the north Indian cities of Varanasi (Kashi), Allahabad (Prayag) and Gaya. Devout Hindus will try to visit these *tirthas* at least once in their life. Varanasi, on the River Ganges, is known as Shiva's city and Hindus who die there are said to achieve instant *moksha*.

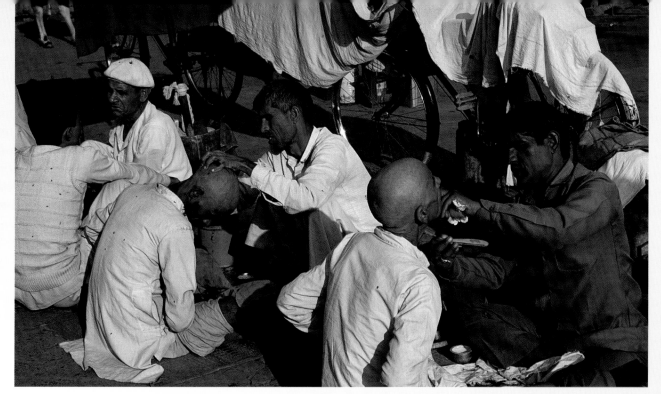

Pilgrims having their heads shaved at the sacred site of Hardwar.

The journey

Before setting out, Hindu pilgrims bathe and pray to cleanse their hearts of bad thoughts. Pilgrims travelling in a group sing and pray together, telling the world of their love for the god they are going to visit. Often they wear white or yellow clothes, colours of renunciation which show that they have left behind ordinary cares and worries.

Are there not many places on this earth? Yet which of them would equal in the balance one speck of Kashi's dust.

Kashi Khanda, 35.7-10

On sacred ground

On arrival at the holy site, the pilgrims bathe again while a pilgrimage priest prays for their sins to be washed away. Next they have their heads shaved, although many women cut only a couple of locks of their hair. Now they are ready to begin visiting the temples at the *tirtha*.

These pilgrims have visited a temple in south India and had their faces marked with the sign of their god.

VARNAS

IN THE PAST, HINDUS WERE divided into four groups called *varnas*: the Brahmins, the Kshatriyas, the Vaishyas and the Sudras. Every Hindu belonged to one of these groups or else was an outcast, an Untouchable.

Jobs and rules

Each *varna* had a particular occupation. The Brahmins were priests and scholars. The Kshatriyas were warriors and kings. The Vaishyas were merchants and the Sudras were farmers and craftsmen. The Untouchables had to perform the dirty jobs, such as cleaning the floor.

These young Brahmin monks can learn the sacred Hindu texts.

Each *varna* had a set of social rules. The Brahmins, who were the purest *varna*, had the strictest rules. They had to be vegetarians, to avoid alcohol and spicy foods, and to accept no food from lower *varnas*.

Lower *varnas* had fewer rules but they were considered impure. Some of the lower *varnas*, for example, were allowed to eat meat.

These Untouchables are working in a leather factory. Working with the products of dead animals, like leather, is considered 'unclean'.

The sacred thread ceremony

In the past, the upper three *varnas* – the Brahmins, Kshatriyas and Vaishyas – had an initiation ceremony, the *Upanayana*, for their children when they were old enough to begin studying. The ceremony was a sign of spiritual rebirth.

This *Upanayana* ceremony still exists. It is now only for boys, but it is not always limited to just the top three *varnas*. In the ceremony, a father hands over his son to a Vedic teacher who ties a cotton thread around him and teaches him the Gayatri Mantra, a prayer from the *Rig Veda*.

Varna today

Varna has been challenged by many Hindus. Nowadays the Indian government has many schemes for educating and employing Untouchables, and officially *varna* no longer determines a Hindu's occupation or social status. Nevertheless, many Untouchables and Sudras remain poor and ill-educated.

This young boy wears the sacred thread.

We meditate on the brilliant light of the One worthy of worship, source of all worlds: may he illuminate our minds.

The Gayatri Mantra, Rig Veda, 3.62.10

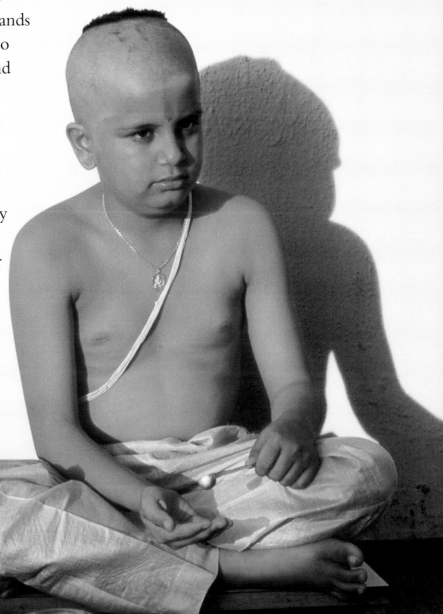

DHARMA: AN IDEAL LIFE

DHARMA IS THE DIVINE ORGANIZATION of things which makes the universe work smoothly as the gods intended. For the divine order to work, people must follow the rules which fit their *varna*, age and sex.

Rules for life

Dharma is religious duty which covers the whole of a person's life. It is a Brahmin's *dharma*, for example, to be a vegetarian and to earn a living as a priest or teacher. It is a child's *dharma* to respect his or her parents and be obedient. *Dharma* requires members of families to look after each other.

The four *ashramas*

A Hindu has four stages to follow in life. These stages, called *ashramas,* come from the Vedas. They are: studenthood, marriage and parenthood, retirement, and renunciation.

In ancient India, both boys and girls were apprenticed for several years to a *guru* (teacher) to study the Vedas. Few teenagers study the Vedas now, but many young Hindus study at modern universities and it is still seen as a time when they should be preparing themselves for the responsibilities of adult life. After their studies, young men and women are expected to get a job,

These children are being taught by their grandmother about the gods and goddesses and the sacred books.

marry and raise a family. The responsibilities of being a householder – of supporting and educating children and caring for elderly relatives – are taken very seriously in Hinduism.

Retiring

Once their children have become independent, a Hindu husband and wife should retire from the world of work and money-making. Many devote more time to prayer and *puja* than they did before.

The final *ashrama* is a time when Hindus prepare themselves for death. Possessions, friends and relations are all abandoned as the elderly person becomes a *sanyasi* – someone who has put aside everything and thinks only of God. Today, few elderly Hindus become total *sanyasis*, but many choose in this final stage of their lives to go on long pilgrimages.

A family gathers outside a temple. Having a family is the second stage of a Hindu's life.

A widow, dressed in white with her hair cut short, takes a bath in the holy River Ganges.

CEREMONIES FOR LIFE

This bride and groom are dressed in the traditional colours of celebration: red and gold.

A boy's head is shaved during his initiation *samskara*.

IN ADDITION TO THE *ASHRAMAS*, Hindus mark their lives by sixteen ceremonies called *samskaras*. These include several ceremonies to welcome new babies into the world, and the *Upanayana* sacred thread ceremony. The two most important are the marriage and funeral rites.

Vivaha: **marriage**

The celebrations for a Hindu wedding may last for days with many grand dinners. At the ceremony itself, the bride is dressed in a gorgeous red and gold sari.

She sits to the left of the groom before a sacred fire, called the *havan* fire. The bride's father offers her to the groom's family while the wedding guests sing songs of blessing. With the bride's right hand on his right shoulder, the groom places ghee and other substances on the fire. Then he leads her in seven steps around the fire, reciting an ancient promise: *Let us love and revere each other, and protect each other with a generous heart; let us see, hear and live a hundred autumns.*

Antyeshti: cremation

The rite of cremation is the last *samskara*. The fire of a cremation pyre is sacred and connects the earthly world with the home of the gods.

The wrapped body is laid on a pile of wood and more wood is placed over it. The pyre is lit. As it burns, offerings of ghee are poured onto it and a prayer is said.

On the third day after the cremation, the family returns to the funeral ground and collects the ashes to scatter them in the River Ganges, or in a nearby river.

Every year afterwards the surviving sons perform a ceremony in which they make offerings of sacred rice balls to their dead ancestors to sustain them on their long journey towards *moksha*.

A body is cremated by the side of a river. Afterwards the ashes from the pyre will be scattered in the river.

IMPORTANT DATES

c.1300BCE The *Rig Veda*, the oldest hymns in Hinduism, begin to be composed.

c.800BCE The epic of the *Mahabharata* begins to be composed. Before it is written down, generations of priests keep it in their memory and teach it to their sons by reciting it to them over and over again.

c.100BCE The story of Lord Rama, the *Ramayana*, is written down in Sanskrit.

600-1600CE The *bhakti* movement flourishes. Instead of paying priests to perform elaborate and expensive sacrifices and rituals, many Hindus begin to worship their gods with simple songs and prayers of love and devotion. Many poets and saints write hymns in the languages which ordinary people speak, such as Hindi, Bengali and Tamil, rather than in Sanskrit.

950-1050 A 'city' of 80 temples is built at Khajuraho, in central India. There are 25 still standing today, which are famous all over the world for their beautiful carvings and sculpture.

1500 The Portuguese establish a small colony in western India to the north of modern Bombay. They begin to tell Europeans about the religion of the Hindus.

c.1580 A north Indian *bhakti* poet, Tulsidas (1532-1623), translates the *Ramayana* from Sanskrit, which is only known by priests and scholars, into Hindi so that ordinary Hindus can understand it. Tulsidas's version is called the *Ramcharitmanas* and is sometimes referred to as 'the Bible of north India'.

1608 The English East India Company builds a warehouse at Surat in west India to buy fine cotton cloth from Indian weavers. This is the start of British power in India; by 1800 the British have defeated many local kings and princes and rule most of the country.

c.1770s European scholars begin translating Hinduism's sacred books into English, German and other European languages.

1833 Ram Mohan Roy (1772-1833), a brilliant teacher from Bengal, dies in Bristol, England. He had come to England to teach politicians and scholars about India and Hindu worship.

1834-1917 Hundreds of thousands of Indian labourers are sent to the West Indies, South Africa, Mauritius, Malaysia and Fiji to work on sugar and rubber plantations and in mines and railways. Wherever they settle, new Hindu communities are created.

1875 Dayananda Saraswati (1824-83) founds the Arya Samaj, a Hindu movement which is against idol-worship and complicated ceremonies. Arya Samajists do not recognize *varna*. It is now a world-wide organization.

1893 Swami Vivekananda (1863-1902), a follower of Lord Rama, represents Hinduism at the World Parliament of Religions in Chicago.

1912 Dr B. R. Ambedkar (1891-1956), from central India, is the first Untouchable to graduate from university. A brilliant lawyer, he eventually becomes Principal of the Government Law College in Bombay and the most important political leader of Untouchables and low-*varna* Hindus.

c.1915 Mohandas Karamchand Gandhi (1869-1948), India's great national leader, begins his non-violent campaign for Indian freedom from British rule. He also tries to get Untouchables treated fairly. Instead of Untouchables, he calls them Harijans, which means 'Children of God'.

1947 India wins independence from the British and part of the Indian sub-continent becomes Pakistan. The new constitution says that all Indians are equal, whatever their religion or *varna*.

1950s-70s Thousands of Indians emigrate to Britain, the USA, Canada and Australia. Hindu communities are formed in these countries and gradually Hindu temples are built.

1965 In America, Swami Prabhupada founds the International Society for Krishna Consciousness, commonly known as the Hare Krishna movement. Members, who can be of any race or nationality, devote themselves to learning about and loving the Hindu god Krishna.

GLOSSARY

Avatar The shapes or forms in which the god Vishnu has visited earth.

Bhagavad Gita The 'Song of the Lord' – the most important Hindu religious text. It is part of the epic *Mahabharata,* and in it, the god Krishna gives advice on daily life.

Cremation The burning of a dead body.

Curd The part of milk which is used to make cheese.

Divine Order The arrangement by the gods of how things should work on earth. 'Divine' means something which comes from the gods.

Epic A long story, often written in verse like a poem, which tells of the deeds of a hero or a famous character like a god.

Ghee Butter that has been purified by melting and straining.

Irreligious Breaking the rules of a religion; being rude about a religion.

Liberation Freedom; being set free.

Mandir A Hindu temple.

Moksha Being set free from the cycle of being born again on earth after death and, instead, becoming one with the Supreme Being.

Murti A holy statue of a god or goddess in a temple that is used for worship.

Puja Hindu worship.

Pyre A pile of wood on which a dead body is burnt in the rite of cremation.

Reincarnation The belief that a person's soul is born again in a new body on earth after death.

Renunciation Giving up, or renouncing, ordinary pleasures and possessions in order to lead a holy life.

Righteousness Good, pure behaviour which obeys the laws of a religion.

Rite A fixed set of rules for a ceremony such as baptism or marriage.

Sacred Holy or religious; something that should be worshipped and respected.

Sacrifice A religious ceremony where something is offered to a god, perhaps an animal like a goat or a sheep.

Sadhu A Hindu holy man.

Sanskrit The ancient language in which the Hindu sacred text are written.

Shaivite Someone who worships Shiva.

Soul The spirit of a person which exists separately from the physical body.

Symbol An object or a picture or a physical movement which stands for something else without having to use exact words to explain it. For example, in Hinduism, the lotus flower is a symbol of beauty and freedom from everyday worries.

Triad A group of three.

Untouchables The group of Hindus who were originally considered to be the lowest part of society, below the four *varnas*.

Vaishnavite Someone who worships Vishnu, or one of his avatars, such as Rama or Krishna.

Varnas The divisions of Hindu society in the past. The four *varnas* were: Brahmins, Kshatriyas, Vaishyas and Sudras.

Vedas Ancient Hindu sacred texts. There are four Vedas.

Vitality The spirit of liveliness and youth.

Yogi A Hindu monk.

INDEX

animals 9, 19, 24, 25
ashramas 26, 27, 28
avatars 12
Ayodhya 11

Bhagavad Gita 10, 13
bhakti-marga 8-9, 30
Bombay 15, 21, 30
Brahma 5
Brahmins 5, 9, 24, 25, 26

ceremonies 8, 28-29;
children 20, 21, 24, 25, 26, 28
colours 23, 27, 28
cows 19
   five sacred products of 19
creation 5, 12, 16
cremation 29

darshan 19
death 6, 15, 27
demons 11, 13
dharma 26-27
Diwali 20
Dussehra 13

families 16, 27, 29
fate *see karma*
festivals 5, 15, 19, 20-21
fire, sacred 4, 29
food 24
funerals 28

Ganesha 14, 15
Ganges, River 9, 11, 14, 22, 27
Gayatri Mantra 25
ghee 5, 19, 20, 29
gods 4, 7, 8, 12, 13, 16-17, 18, 19, 22, 23, 29
Goddess, Great *see* Mahadevi
goddesses 4, 12, 15
gopis 13
guru 26

Hanuman 11
head shaving 23, 28
Holi 20, 21
Holika 21
holy books *see* sacred texts
hymns 8, 9, 10, 30

Kabir 9
Kali 15
Kalighat 15
Kansa 13
karma 6, 7
Kauravas 10
Krishna 9, 10, 12, 13
Kshatriyas 5, 24, 25

Lakshman 12, 20
Lakshmi 12, 20
lamps 5, 16, 20

Mahabharata 10, 11, 30
Mahadevi, Great Goddess 15
marriage 26, 27, 28-29
moksha 7, 22, 29
monks 14, 17, 25
murtis 16

offerings 8, 9, 18

Parvati 14, 15
pilgrims/pilgrimage 7, 17, 22-23, 27
prasad 18
prayer 6, 7, 8, 9, 10, 17, 19, 27
priests 5, 8, 9, 16, 17, 18, 19, 23, 24, 26, 30
puja 6, 7, 18-19, 27
Rama 5, 9, 11, 12, 13, 30
Ramayana 10, 11, 13, 30
Ravana 11, 13
rebirth 6, 7,

Rig Veda 10, 25, 30
sacred texts 5, 9, 10-11, 25
sacrifices 8, 30; *see also* offerings
samskaras 28-29
Sanskrit 9, 10, 11, 30
sanyasi 27
Shakti *see* Mahadevi
Shiva 5, 14, 15, 22
shrines 16, 18
Supreme Being 4, 7, 12, 22
Sudras 5, 24, 25

teacher, religious 8, 25, 26
temples 4, 5, 12, 15, 16-17, 18,   19, 22, 23, 27, 30
   bell 17
tirthas 22, 23
Triad, the 5

universe 4, 5, 6, 12, 14, 16
Untouchables 5, 24, 25, 30
Upanayana 25, 28

Vaishnavites 12, 13
Vaishyas 5, 24, 25
varnas 5, 8, 9, 24-25, 26, 28
Vedas 10, 11, 25, 26
vegetarians 9, 24, 26
vivaha 28-29
Vishnu 5, 12-13

water 22
Way of Devotion *see* bhakti-marga
worship *see puja*

yoga 7
yogi 14